Arentine H. Arendsen's Dutch Flowers:

A Vintage Grayscale Adult Coloring Book

By Ligia Ortega

ColoringPress.com

This book is dedicated to Jill. Thank you for your encouragement, kindness, and for the enthusiasm you share.

ARTIST'S MESSAGE

It means so much that you have chosen to purchase this book. I hope it brings you or a loved one hours of coloring pleasure.

All images in this book were lovingly sourced, curated, and restored by me. I then worked to carefully convert every image to high-quality colorable grayscale, digitize every page and assemble them electronically to prepare for printing. This coloring book has been a true labor of love, representing months of work (plus sleep deprivation and neglect of friendships and housework!). Although the source images are public domain, the work I have done to restore and convert these images into grayscale coloring pages is protected by Copyright Law. I took the time and additional expense to officially register this book with the Copyright Office. Please respect Copyright Law.

You may:

Copy the uncolored pages on other paper preferences for yourself.
Post colored images on social media.
Give the colored pages as gifts.
Give a physical book you purchased as a gift.

You may not:

Share physical or electronic copies of uncolored pages with anyone else, whether free or for sale.
Post uncolored pages anywhere online, claim them as your own, or distribute uncolored pages via e-mail or electronic downloads.
Incorporate uncolored or colored images on items besides colored pages.
Sell uncolored or colored images, cards, or crafts made with the coloring pages, use them on products, or for any commercial usage.

ColoringGifts@yahoo.com   ColoringPress.com   www.facebook.com/ColoringPress

ISBN: 9781731532428

THIS BOOK BELONGS TO:

_____

ABOUT THIS BOOK

Early in my art career I was exposed to the work of several turn-of-the-century illustrators, and I discovered a few favorites whose work I spent hours poring over. This all happened in the days before the internet, so finding work by these artists took some dedicated searching. The local library didn't have anything and I finally found myself digging around the stacks of the local university's fine arts library, giddy to find books of their work. I was delighted a few years later when I enrolled and was finally able to get a library card for the university's library because it meant I could actually bring some of these books home with me instead of spending hours at library stacks looking at illustrations.

While working on other adult coloring books, I remembered these illustrations I loved so much, and thought wouldn't it be wonderful to take the exquisite work done by this amazing illustrator and introduce it to a whole new generation of people? I got to work and began researching, sourcing illustrations, curating them to the best ones, and spent hours sorting them into several collections. Then the real work began. These illustrations could not be separated from the original technique and rather than being converted to line art, the best way to maintain the integrity of these works would be to let them have the nuances of grayscale. I worked to restore the illustrations (the originals I was able to source for this book were more than 140 years old, so they needed hours of work to be made into this finished book) and then finally digitizing the images to get them ready to print. I researched and learned how to make the best possible colorable grayscale page (it's a lot more complex than simply making an image black and white) and after converting the restored, digitized illustrations to grayscale, set out to assemble the images into this book. This is the fourth book in a series, and I will be working on more vintage grayscale adult coloring books showcasing my favorite vintage artists and illustrators.

Arentina Hendrica Arendsen (1836-1915) was a Dutch painter and botanical illustrator known for her beautiful still life paintings featuring flowers and bulbs of her era. Her original paintings are still popular today when they come up for auction. She was born in Amsterdam and died in Haarlem.

I am already working on the next volume of my vintage grayscale adult coloring book series. Please visit my site at ColoringPress.com or find me on Facebook at facebook.com/ColoringPress to share your colored pages, to get grayscale coloring tips, and for more information on my next volumes in this series.

Thank you for choosing this volume and I hope you enjoy coloring Arentine Arendsen's beautiful flowers!

Ligia Ortega

AMARYLLIS BELLADONNA.

Arentine H Arendsen ad nat del.

Arentine H. Arendsen's Dutch Flowers

EUCHARIS AMAZONICA.

Arentine H. Arendsen ad nat. del.

RICHARDIA AFRICANA CALLA AETHIOPICA ARUM AETHIOPICUM)

Arentine H. Arendsen's Dutch Flowers

Arentine H Arendsen ad nat del

COLCHICUM BYZANTINUM, VARR.

Arentine H. Arendsen's Dutch Flowers

CROCUS VERNUS. VAR.

DOUBLE NARCISSUS

Arentine H. Arendsen's Dutch Flowers

DOUBLE TULIPS

Arentine H. Arendsen ad nat del

Arentine H. Arendsen's Dutch Flowers

SINGLE DUC VAN THOLL TULIPS

Arentine H. Arendsen ad nat. del.

Arentine H. Arendsen's Dutch Flowers

LILIUM LONGIFLORUM.

Arentine H Arendsen ad nat del

Arentine H. Arendsen's Dutch Flowers

GLADIOLUS. DWARF HYBRIDS

Arentine H Arendsen ad nat del

HYACINTHS.

Arentine H. Arendsen ad. nat. del.

Arentine H. Arendsen's Dutch Flowers

Arentine H. Arendsen's Dutch Flowers

HYACINTHUS CANDICANS.

Arentine H. Arendsen's Dutch Flowers

IRIS GERMANICA : VARR.

Arentine H. Arendsen's Dutch Flowers

IRIS KAEMPFERI. VAR:

Arentine H. Arendsen, ad nat del.

Arentine H. Arendsen's Dutch Flowers

LILIUM AURATUM.

Arentine H. Arendsen ad nat del

Arentine H. Arendsen's Dutch Flowers

© Ligia Ortega - ColoringPress.com

LILIUM BROWNII.

Arentine H. Arendsen ad nat del

LILIUM CANDIDUM

Arentine H Arendsen ad.nat del.

Arentine H. Arendsen's Dutch Flowers

LILIUM SPECIOSUM ALBUM (LANCIFOLIUM ALBUM.)

Arentine H. Arendsen's Dutch Flowers

Arentine H. Arendsen ad.nat.del.

LILIUM SPECIOSUM RUBRUM (LANCIFOLIUM RUBRUM)

Arentine H. Arendsen's Dutch Flowers

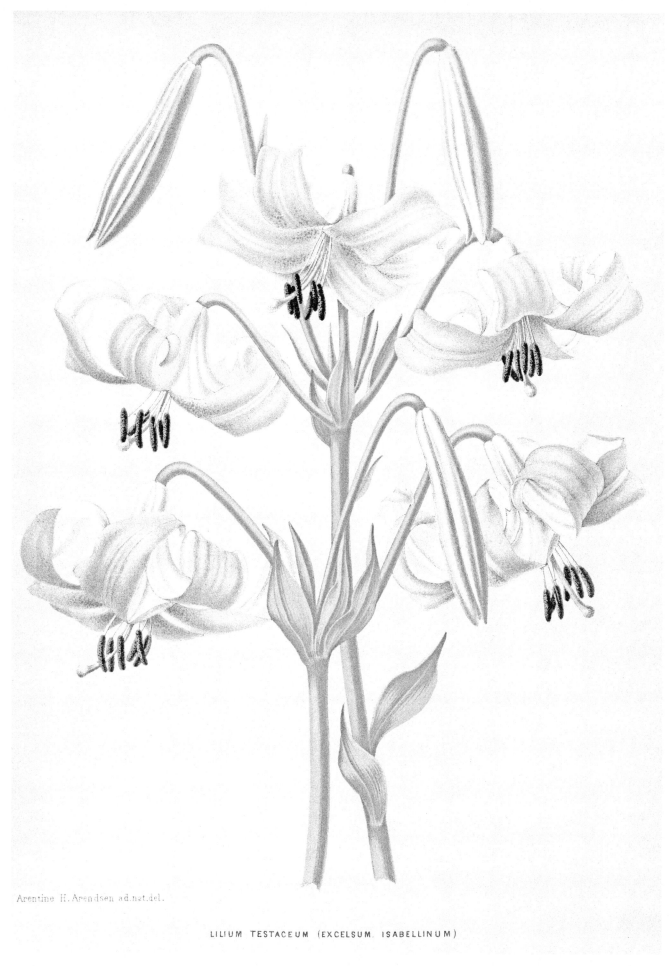

LILIUM TESTACEUM (EXCELSUM. ISABELLINUM)

Arentine H. Arendsen ad.nat.del.

Arentine H. Arendsen's Dutch Flowers

© Ligia Ortega - ColoringPress.com

Arentine H.Arendsen ad.nat.del.

LILIUM THUNBERGIANUM VENUSTUM. (L.VENUSTUM)

Arentine H. Arendsen's Dutch Flowers

© Ligia Ortega - ColoringPress.com

LILIUM THUNBERGIANUM AUREUM MACULATUM

Arentine H Arendsen ad nat del.

Arentine H. Arendsen's Dutch Flowers

LILIUM UMBELLATUM INCOMPARABILE.

Arentine H Arendsen ad nat del

NARCISSUS

Arentine H. Arendsen ad.nat.del.

Arentine H. Arendsen's Dutch Flowers

NARCISSUS.

Arentine H. Arendsen ad. nat. del.

NARCISSUS.

Arentine H. Arendsen's Dutch Flowers

NARCISSUS.

Arentine H. Arendsen ad nat del.

Arentine H. Arendsen's Dutch Flowers

Arentine H Arendsen ad nat del.

1. NARCISSUS BICOLOR. 2. NARCISSUS BICOLOR VAR HORSFIELDI

Arentine H. Arendsen ad nat. del.

PANCRATIUM ILLYRICUM.

Arentine H. Arendsen's Dutch Flowers

© Ligia Ortega - ColoringPress.com

Arentine H. Arendsen ad nat del.

ALSTROEMERIA CHILENSIS, VARR.

Arentine H. Arendsen's Dutch Flowers

POLYANTHUS NARCISSUS.

Aréntine H Arendsen ad nat

POLYANTHUS NARCISSUS

Arentine H. Arendsen ad nat. del

SINGLE EARLY TULIP, LA LAITIÈRE

Arentine H. Arendsen ad. nat. del.

Arentine H. Arendsen's Dutch Flowers

SINGLE EARLY TULIPS.

Arentine H. Arendsen's Dutch Flowers

SINGLE EARLY TULIPS.

Arentine H Arendsen ad nat del

SINGLE EARLY TULIPS

Arentine H Arendsen ad nat del.

SINGLE EARLY TULIPS.

Arentine H. Arendsen's Dutch Flowers

SINGLE EARLY TULIP

Bonus Pages

In addition to the *Vintage Grayscale Adult Coloring Book* series, I have been working on other coloring books for adults. The following coloring pages are from books I have published under Coloring Press.

The first images are samples from Volumes 1-3 of my *Vintage Grayscale Adult Coloring Book* Series, Volume 1 *Arthur Rackham's Fairies and Nymphs,* Volume 2, *Warwick Goble's Fairy Tales,* and Volume 3, *Bevalet's Hummingbirds and Flowers.* I am already working on Volume 5 of this series. Visit ColoringPress.com for more information on grayscale coloring.

The remaining images are from my *Simple Kaleidoscopes* and *Simple Mandalas* coloring books. I took on the challenge of making kaleidoscopes and mandalas by hand rather than having software generated ones. It was fun watching them come to life from my own hand-drawn black and white coloring images. These kaleidoscopes and mandalas are published as full size 8.5x11" books and also as travel size 6x8" books. I published these books in response to colorists asking for a less intricate kaleidoscope and mandala where they could show off their shading or just have larger spaces to color. Their bold lines and larger spaces also work well for people with low vision or issues with hand control. The travel size books, *Pocket Kaleidoscopes* and *Pocket Mandalas* are perfect for taking with you to the mechanic, the dentist, the doctor's office, or any place where you may have to wait. They make the time fly by quickly and the wait a lot more pleasant, and their small size means you can usually finish coloring a page in one sitting. The repetitive patterns are relaxing and fun to color and I have heard from colorists that they help with anxiety, insomnia, PTSD, and more. This series is being well received by colorists and I will be publishing additional Simple books in different themes.

Arthur Rackham's Fairies and Nymphs

Bevalet's Hummingbirds and Flowers

TEST & RECORD YOUR FAVORITE PALETTES & COLOR COMBINATIONS!

The Colorist Palette Reference Book works as a place to:
- keep track of your favorite color combinations
- test drive new media
- help you remember what supplies you were using if you have to pack them
  up /put them away before you finish coloring a page
- test and practice new techniques before you work on a coloring page
- experiment with new palettes to see if the colors play together nicely
- keep track of colors you used on a coloring page

The book has 48 full size pages in 12 different designs.
There is a small simple picture on the top half of each page and the bottom has space for swatches and lines for recording color and/or media that you used, or to take notes or keep track of blending.
The image does not have to be colored fully, it's there to see how the colors go together or for you to try new techniques. There is blank space too for notes about which coloring page you used the particular palette, media, or technique on.
This book came out of my own needs as a colorist, so I hope it will be useful! This book does not have colored pages, they are blank so you can record your own favorite palettes, combinations, or notes.

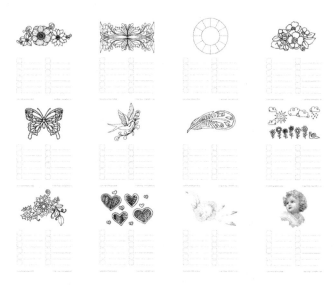

The 12 designs in the book

MEDITATIVE COLORING - WITH A PURPOSE!

These themed adult coloring books are great to have on hand for when life calls for encouragement, showing gratitude, or appreciation to friends. Each book in the Coloring Gifts™ Book Series includes:
- 24 original hand drawn coloring pages
- Each single sided page is printed in two different sizes: full size and craft size, approx. 5x7"
- Nine coordinating bookmarks
- Instructions on how to add special touches to your Coloring Gifts™
- Pages can be colored and given as is, or framed, made into cards, or made into bookmarks to give as gifts
- Coloring these pages can be done as a prayer or meditation aid with the included themed lists of scriptures and instructions for meditation to help you reap the full health benefits of coloring and gratitude, encouragement, and friendship.

COLORING GIFTS™ BOOKS - AVAILABLE ON AMAZON & BOOK DEPOSITORY

Coloring Gifts™: Gifts of Thanks

Coloring Gifts™: Gifts of Encouragement

Coloring Gifts™: Gifts of Friendship

I hope you enjoyed Arentine H. Arendsen's Dutch Flowers!

Please take a moment to leave a review on the book's Amazon page.

To find other volumes of Vintage Grayscale Adult Coloring Books, for grayscale coloring tips, to share your colored pages on Facebook, and to find my other adult coloring books, please visit:

ColoringPress.com

Made in the USA
Monee, IL
03 December 2019